DEPARTMENT OF THE NAVY
HEADQUARTERS UNITED STATES MARINE CORPS
3000 MARINE CORPS PENTAGON
WASHINGTON, D.C. 20350-3000

GROUND SENSOR SURVEILLANCE TRAINING AND READINESS MANUAL

DEPARTMENT OF THE NAVY
HEADQUARTERS UNITED STATES MARINE CORPS
3000 MARINE CORPS PENTAGON
WASHINGTON, D.C. 20350-3000

NAVMC 3500.17A
C 469
8 Sep 2010

NAVMC 3500.17A

From: Commandant of the Marine Corps
To: Distribution List

Subj: GROUND SENSOR SURVEILLANCE TRAINING AND READINESS MANUAL, (SHORT
       TITLE: GROUND SENSOR T&R MANUAL)

Encl: (a) MCO P3500.72A
       (b) MCO 1553.3A
       (c) MCO 3400.3F
       (d) MCO 3500.27B W/Erratum
       (e) MCRP 3-0A
       (f) MCRP 3-0B
       (g) MCO 1553.2B

1. Purpose. Per reference (a), this T&R Manual establishes required events for standardized training of Marines and Navy personnel assigned to perform Ground Sensor Surveillance functions. Additionally, it provides tasking for formal schools preparing personnel for service in the Marine Corps Ground Sensor Surveillance community. This NAVMC supersedes NAVMC 3500.17.

2. Scope

    a. Per reference (b), commanders will conduct an internal assessment of the unit's ability, and develop long-, mid-, and short-range training plans to sustain proficiency. Training plans will incorporate these events to standardize training and provide objective assessment of progress toward attaining combat readiness. Commanders will keep records at the unit and individual levels to record training achievements, identify training gaps, and document objective assessments of readiness associated with training Marines. Commanders will use reference (c) to incorporate nuclear, biological, and chemical defense training into training plans and reference (d) to integrate operational risk management. References (e) and (f) provide amplifying information for effective planning and management of training within the unit.

    b. Formal school and training detachment commanders will use references (a) and (g) to ensure programs of instruction meet skill training requirements established in this manual, and provide career-progression training in the events designated for initial training in the formal school environment.

3. Information. CG, TECOM will update this T&R Manual as necessary to provide current and relevant training standards to commanders. All questions pertaining to the Marine Corps Ground T&R Program and Unit Training Management should be directed to: Commanding General, TECOM (Ground Training Division C 469), 1019 Elliot Road, Quantico, VA 22134.

4. <u>Command</u>. This Directive is applicable to the Marine Corps Total Force.

5. <u>Certification</u>. Reviewed and approved this date.

R. C. FOX
By direction

Distribution: PCN 10033195300

    Copy to: 7000260 (2)
              8145001 (1)

LOCATOR SHEET

Subj: GROUND SENSOR SURVEILLANCE TRAINING AND READINESS MANUAL, (SHORT
        TITLE: GROUND SENSOR T&R MANUAL)

Location: _____

                (Indicate location(s) of copy(ies) of this Manual.)

RECORD OF CHANGES

Log completed change action as indicated.

Change Number	Date of Change	Date Entered	Signature of Person Incorporated Change

GROUND SENSOR T&R MANUAL

TABLE OF CONTENTS

GROUND SENSOR T&R MANUAL

CHAPTER 1

OVERVIEW

CHAPTER 1

OVERVIEW

1000. INTRODUCTION

1. The T&R Program is the Corps' primary tool for planning, conducting and evaluating training and assessing training readiness. Subject Matter Experts (SMEs) from the operating forces developed core capability Mission Essential Task Lists (METLs) for ground communities derived from the Marine Corps Task List (MCTL). T&R Manuals are built around these METLs and all events contained in T&R Manuals relate directly to this METL. This comprehensive T&R Program will help to ensure the Marine Corps continues to improve its combat readiness by training more efficiently and effectively. Ultimately, this will enhance the Marine Corps' ability to accomplish real-world missions.

2. The T&R Manual contains the individual and collective training requirements to prepare the Ground Sensor Surveillance community to accomplish their mission. The T&R Manual is not intended to be an encyclopedia that contains every minute detail of how to accomplish training. Instead, it identifies the minimum standards that Marines must be able to perform in their MOS. The T&R Manual is a fundamental tool for commanders to build and maintain unit readiness. Using this tool, leaders can construct and execute an effective training plan that supports the unit's METL. More detailed information on the Marine Corps Ground T&R Program is found in reference (a).

1001. UNIT TRAINING

1. The training of Marines to perform as an integrated unit in combat lies at the heart of the T&R program. Unit and individual readiness are directly related. Individual training and the mastery of individual core skills serve as the building blocks for unit readiness. A Marine's ability to perform critical skills required is essential. However, it is not necessary to have all individuals within a unit fully trained in order for that organization to accomplish its assigned tasks. Manpower shortfalls, temporary assignments, leave, or other factors outside the commander's control, often affect the ability to conduct individual training. During these periods, unit readiness is enhanced if emphasis is placed on the individual training of Marines on-hand. Subsequently, these Marines will be mission ready and capable of executing as part of a team when the full complement of personnel is available.

2. Commanders will ensure that all tactical training is focused on their combat mission. The T&R Manual is a tool to help develop the unit's training plan. In most cases, unit training should focus on achieving unit proficiency in the core capabilities METL. However, commanders will adjust their training focus to support METLs associated with a major OPLAN/CONPLAN or named operation as designated by their higher commander and reported

accordingly in the Defense Readiness Reporting System (DRRS). Tactical training will support the METL in use by the commander and be tailored to meet T&R standards. Commanders at all levels are responsible for effective training. The conduct of training in a professional manner consistent with Marine Corps standards cannot be over emphasized.

3. Commanders will provide personnel the opportunity to attend formal and operational level courses of instruction as required by this Manual. Attendance at all formal courses must enhance the warfighting capabilities of the unit as determined by the unit commander.

1002. UNIT TRAINING MANAGEMENT

1. Unit Training Management (UTM) is the application of the Systems Approach to Training (SAT) and the Marine Corps Training Principles. This is accomplished in a manner that maximizes training results and focuses the training priorities of the unit in preparation for the conduct of its wartime mission.

2. UTM techniques, described in references (b) and (e), provide commanders with the requisite tools and techniques to analyze, design, develop, implement, and evaluate the training of their unit. The Marine Corps Training Principles, explained in reference (b), provide sound and proven direction and are flexible enough to accommodate the demands of local conditions. These principles are not inclusive, nor do they guarantee success. They are guides that commanders can use to manage unit-training programs. The Marine Corps training principles are:

- Train as you fight
- Make commanders responsible for training
- Use standards-based training
- Use performance-oriented training
- Use mission-oriented training
- Train the MAGTF to fight as a combined arms team
- Train to sustain proficiency
- Train to challenge

3. To maintain an efficient and effective training program, leaders at every level must understand and implement UTM. Guidance for UTM and the process for establishing effective programs are contained in references (a) through (g).

1003. SUSTAINMENT AND EVALUATION OF TRAINING

1. The evaluation of training is necessary to properly prepare Marines for their mission. Evaluations are either formal or informal, and performed by members of the unit (internal evaluation) or from an external command (external evaluation).

2. Marines are expected to maintain proficiency in the training events for their MOS at the appropriate grade or billet to which assigned. Leaders are responsible for recording the training achievements of their Marines. Whether it involves individual or collective training events, they must

ensure proficiency is sustained by requiring retraining of each event at or before expiration of the designated sustainment interval. Performance of the training event, however, is not sufficient to ensure readiness. Leaders at all levels must evaluate the performance of their Marines and the unit as they complete training events, and only record successful accomplishment of training based upon the evaluation. The goal of evaluation is to ensure that correct methods are employed to achieve the desired standard, or the Marines understand how they need to improve in order to attain the standard. Leaders must determine whether credit for completing a training event is recorded if the standard was not achieved. While successful accomplishment is desired, debriefing of errors can result in successful learning that will allow ethical recording of training event completion. Evaluation is a continuous process that is integral to training management and is conducted by leaders at every level and during all phases of planning and the conduct of training. To ensure training is efficient and effective, evaluation is an integral part of the training plan. Ultimately, leaders remain responsible for determining if the training was effective.

3. The purpose of formal and informal evaluation is to provide commanders with a process to determine a unit's/Marine's proficiency in the tasks that must be performed. Informal evaluations are conducted during every training evolution. Formal evaluations are often scenario-based, focused on the unit's METs, based on collective training standards, and usually conducted during higher-level collective events. References (a) and (f) provide further guidance on the conduct of informal and formal evaluations using the Marine Corps Ground T&R Program.

1004. ORGANIZATION

1. T&R Manuals are organized in one of two methods: unit-based or community-based. Unit-based T&R Manuals are written to support a type of unit (Infantry, Artillery, Tanks, etc.) and contain both collective and individual training standards. Community-based are written to support an Occupational Field, a group of related Military Occupational Specialties (MOSs), or billets within an organization (EOD, Intel, Ground Sensor Surveillance, etc.), and usually only contain individual training standards. T&R Manuals are comprised of chapters that contain unit METs, collective training standards (CTS), and individual training standards (ITS) for each MOS, billet, etc.

2. The Ground Sensor Surveillance T&R Manual is an community-based manual comprised of 4 chapters. Chapter 2 lists the Core Capability METs. Chapter 3 list collective events and chapter 4 contains the individual events.

1005. T&R EVENT CODING

1. T&R events are coded for ease of reference. Each event has a 4-4-4-digit identifier. The first four digits are referred to as a "community" and represent the unit type or occupation (GRSO and 8621). The second four digits represent the functional or duty area (DISS, PLAN, RESO, etc.). The last four digits represent the level and sequence of the event.

2. The T&R levels are illustrated in Figure 1. An example of the T&R coding used in this Manual is shown in Figure 2.

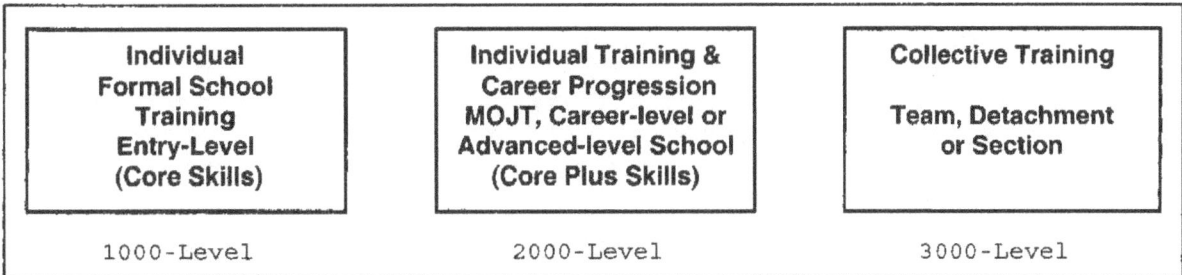

Figure 1: T&R Event Levels

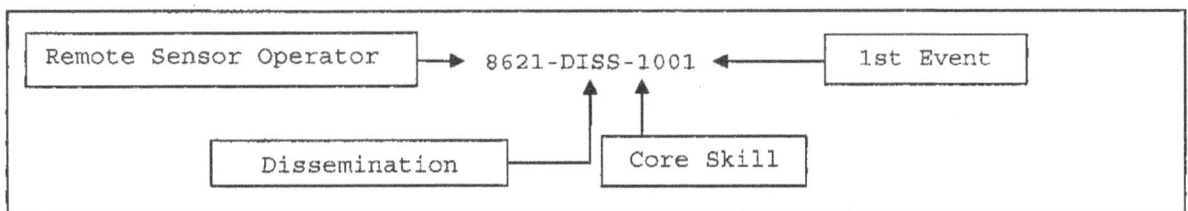

Figure 2: T&R Event Coding

1006. COMBAT READINESS PERCENTAGE

1. The Marine Corps Ground T&R Program includes processes to assess readiness of units and individual Marines. Every unit in the Marine Corps maintains a basic level of readiness based on the training and experience of the Marines in the unit. Even units that never trained together are capable of accomplishing some portion of their missions. Combat readiness assessment does not associate a quantitative value for this baseline of readiness, but uses a "Combat Readiness Percentage", as a method to provide a concise descriptor of the recent training accomplishments of units and Marines.

2. Combat Readiness Percentage (CRP) is the percentage of required training events that a unit or Marine accomplishes within specified sustainment intervals.

3. In unit-based T&R Manuals, unit combat readiness is assessed as a percentage of the successfully completed and current (within sustainment interval) key training events called "Evaluation-Coded" (E-Coded) Events. E-Coded Events and unit CRP calculation are described in follow-on paragraphs. CRP achieved through the completion of E-Coded Events is directly relevant to readiness assessment in DRRS.

4. Individual combat readiness, in both unit-based and community-based T&R Manuals, is assessed as the percentage of required individual events in which a Marine is current. This translates as the percentage of training events for his/her MOS and grade (or billet) that the Marine successfully completes within the directed sustainment interval. Individual skills are developed through a combination of 1000-level training (entry-level formal school courses), individual on-the-job training in 2000-level events, and follow-on

formal school training. Skill proficiency is maintained by retraining in each event per the specified sustainment interval.

1007. EVALUATION-CODED (E-CODED) EVENTS

1. Unit-type T&R Manuals can contain numerous unit events, some for the whole unit and others for integral parts that serve as building blocks for training. To simplify training management and readiness assessment, only collective events that are critical components of a mission essential task (MET), or key indicators of a unit's readiness, are used to generate CRP for a MET. These critical or key events are designated in the T&R Manual as Evaluation-Coded (E-Coded) events. Formal evaluation of unit performance in these events is recommended because of their value in assessing combat readiness. Only E-Coded events are used to calculate CRP for each MET.

2. The use of a METL-based training program allows the commander discretion in training. This makes the T&R Manual a training tool rather than a prescriptive checklist.

1008. CRP CALCULATION

1. Collective training begins at the 3000 level (team, crew or equivalent). Unit training plans are designed to accomplish the events that support the unit METL while simultaneously sustaining proficiency in individual core skills. Using the battalion-based (unit) model, the battalion (7000-level) has collective events that directly support a MET on the METL. These collective events are E-Coded and the only events that contribute to unit CRP. This is done to assist commanders in prioritizing the training toward the METL, taking into account resource, time, and personnel constraints.

2. Unit CRP increases after the completion of E-Coded events. The number of E-Coded events for the MET determines the value of each E-Coded event. For example, if there are 4 E-Coded events for a MET, each is worth 25% of MET CRP. MET CRP is calculated by adding the percentage of each completed and current (within sustainment interval) E-Coded training event. The percentage for each MET is calculated the same way and all are added together and divided by the number of METS to determine unit CRP. For ease of calculation, we will say that each MET has 4 E-Coded events, each contributing 25% towards the completion of the MET. If the unit has completed and is current on three of the four E-Coded events for a given MET, then they have completed 75% of the MET. The CRP for each MET is added together and divided by the number of METS to get unit CRP; unit CRP is the average of MET CRP.

For Example:

```
MET 1:  75% complete  (3 of 4 E-Coded events trained)
MET 2:  100% complete (6 of 6 E-Coded events trained)
MET 3:  25% complete  (1 of 4 E-Coded events trained)
MET 4:  50% complete  (2 of 4 E-Coded events trained)
MET 5:  75% complete  (3 of 4 E-Coded events trained)
```

To get unit CRP, simply add the CRP for each MET and divide by the number of METS:

MET CRP: 75 + 100 + 25 + 50 + 75 = 325

Unit CRP: 325 (total MET CRP)/ 5 (total number of METS) = 65%

1009. T&R EVENT COMPOSITION

1. This section explains each of the components of a T&R event. These items are included in all events in each T&R manual.

   a. Event Code (see Sect 1006). The event code is a 4-4-4 character set. For individual training events, the first 4 characters indicate the occupational function. The second 4 characters indicate functional area (TAC, CBTS, VOPS, etc.). The third 4 characters are simply a numerical designator for the event.

   b. Event Title. The event title is the name of the event.

   c. E-Coded. This is a "yes/no" category to indicate whether or not the event is E-Coded. If yes, the event contributes toward the CRP of the associated MET. The value of each E-Coded event is based on number of E-Coded events for that MET. Refer to paragraph 1008 for detailed explanation of E-Coded events.

   d. Supported MET(s). List all METs that are supported by the training event.

   e. Sustainment Interval. This is the period, expressed in number of months, between evaluation or retraining requirements. Skills and capabilities acquired through the accomplishment of training events are refreshed at pre-determined intervals. It is essential that these intervals are adhered to in order to ensure Marines maintain proficiency.

   f. Billet. Individual training events may contain a list of billets within the community that are responsible for performing that event. This ensures that the billet's expected tasks are clearly articulated and a Marine's readiness to perform in that billet is measured.

   g. Grade. Each individual training event will list the rank(s) at which Marines are required to learn and sustain the training event.

   h. Initial Training Setting. For Individual T&R Events only, this specifies the location for initial instruction of the training event in one of three categories (formal school, managed on-the-job training, distance learning). Regardless of the specified Initial Training Setting, any T&R event may be introduced and evaluated during managed on-the-job training.

      (1) "FORMAL" - When the Initial Training Setting of an event is identified as "FORMAL" (formal school), the appropriate formal school or training detachment is required to provide initial training in the event. Conversely, formal schools and training detachments are not authorized to provide training in events designated as Initial Training Setting "MOJT" or

"DL." Since the duration of formal school training must be constrained to optimize Operating Forces' manning, this element provides the mechanism for Operating Forces' prioritization of training requirements for both entry-level (1000-level) and career-level (2000-level) T&R Events. For formal schools and training detachments, this element defines the requirements for content of courses.

       (2) "DL" - Identifies the training event as a candidate for initial training via a Distance Learning product (correspondence course or MarineNet course).

       (3) "MOJT" - Events specified for Managed On-the-Job Training are to be introduced to Marines, and evaluated, as part of training within a unit by supervisory personnel.

   i. Event Description. Provide a description of the event purpose, objectives, goals, and requirements. It is a general description of an action requiring learned skills and knowledge (e.g. Camouflage the M1A1 Tank).

   j. Condition. Describe the condition(s), under which tasks are performed. Conditions are based on a "real world" operational environment. They indicate what is provided (equipment, materials, manuals, aids, etc.), environmental constraints, conditions under which the task is performed, and any specific cues or indicators to which the performer must respond. When resources or safety requirements limit the conditions, this is stated.

   k. Standard. The standard indicates the basis for judging effectiveness of the performance. It consists of a carefully worded statement that identifies the proficiency level expected when the task is performed. The standard provides the minimum acceptable performance parameters and is strictly adhered to. The standard for collective events is general, describing the desired end-state or purpose of the event. While the standard for individual events specifically describe to what proficiency level in terms of accuracy, speed, sequencing, quality of performance, adherence to procedural guidelines, etc., the event is accomplished.

   l. Event Components. Describe the actions composing the event and help the user determine what must be accomplished and to properly plan for the event.

   m. Prerequisite Events. Prerequisites are academic training or other T&R events that must be completed prior to attempting the task. They are lower-level events or tasks that give the individual/unit the skills required to accomplish the event. They can also be planning steps, administrative requirements, or specific parameters that build toward mission accomplishment.

   n. Chained Events. Collective T&R events are supported by lower-level collective and individual T&R events. This enables unit leaders to effectively identify subordinate T&R events that ultimately support specific mission essential tasks. When the accomplishment of any upper-level events, by their nature, result in the performance of certain subordinate and related events, the events are "chained." The completion of chained events will update sustainment interval credit (and CRP for E-Coded events) for the related subordinate level events.

    o. Related Events. Provide a list of all Individual Training Standards that support the event.

    p. References. The training references are utilized to determine task performance steps, grading criteria, and ensure standardization of training procedures. They assist the trainee in satisfying the performance standards, or the trainer in evaluating the effectiveness of task completion. References are also important to the development of detailed training plans.

    q. Distance Learning Products (IMI, CBT, MCI, etc.). Include this component when the event can be taught via one of these media methods vice attending a formal course of instruction or receiving MOJT.

    r. Support Requirements. This is a list of the external and internal support the unit and Marines will need to complete the event. The list includes, but is not limited to:

- Range(s)/Training Area
- Ordnance
- Equipment
- Materials
- Other Units/Personnel
- Other Support Requirements

    s. Miscellaneous. Provide any additional information that assists in the planning and execution of the event. Miscellaneous information may include, but is not limited to:

- Admin Instructions
- Special Personnel Certifications
- Equipment Operating Hours
- Road Miles

2. Community-based T&R manuals have several additional components not found in unit-based T&R manuals. These additions do not apply to this T&R Manual.

1010. CBRND TRAINING

1. All personnel assigned to the operating force must be trained in chemical, biological, radiological, and nuclear defense (CBRND), in order to survive and continue their mission in a CBRN environment. Individual proficiency standards are defined as survival and basic operating standards. Survival standards are those that the individual must master in order to survive a CBRN incident. Basic operating standards are those that the individual, and collectively the unit, must perform to continue operations in a CBRND environment.

2. CBRN Officers and Specialists are instrumental in integrating realistic scenarios/situations that challenge units' ability to operate in a CBRN environment. Units should train under CBRND conditions whenever possible.

Per reference (c), all units must be capable of accomplishing their assigned mission in a contaminated environment.

1011. NIGHT TRAINING

1. While it is understood that all personnel and units of the operating force are capable of performing their assigned mission in "every climate and place," current doctrine emphasizes the requirement to perform assigned missions at night and during periods of limited visibility. Basic skills are significantly more difficult when visibility is limited.

2. To ensure units are capable of accomplishing their mission they must train under the conditions of limited visibility. Units should strive to conduct all events in this T&R Manual during both day and night/limited visibility conditions. When there is limited training time available, night training should take precedence over daylight training, contingent on individual, crew, and unit proficiency.

1012. OPERATIONAL RISK MANAGEMENT (ORM)

1. ORM is a process that enables commanders to plan for and minimize risk while still accomplishing the mission. It is a decision making tool used by Marines at all levels to increase operational effectiveness by anticipating hazards and reducing the potential for loss, thereby increasing the probability of a successful mission. ORM minimizes risks to acceptable levels, commensurate with mission accomplishment.

2. Commanders, leaders, maintainers, planners, and schedulers will integrate risk assessment in the decision-making process and implement hazard controls to reduce risk to acceptable levels. Applying the ORM process will reduce mishaps, lower costs, and provide for more efficient use of resources. ORM assists the commander in conserving lives and resources and avoiding unnecessary risk, making an informed decision to implement a course of action (COA), identifying feasible and effective control measures where specific measures do not exist, and providing reasonable alternatives for mission accomplishment. Most importantly, ORM assists the commander in determining the balance between training realism and unnecessary risks in training, the impact of training operations on the environment, and the adjustment of training plans to fit the level of proficiency and experience of Sailors/Marines and leaders. Further guidance for ORM is found in references (b) and (d).

1013. APPLICATION OF SIMULATION

1. Simulations/Simulators and other training devices shall be used when they are capable of effectively and economically supplementing training on the identified training task. Particular emphasis shall be placed on simulators that provide training that might be limited by safety considerations or constraints on training space, time, or other resources. When deciding on simulation issues, the primary consideration shall be improving the quality of training and consequently the state of readiness. Potential savings in

operating and support costs normally shall be an important secondary consideration.

2. Each training event contains information relating to the applicability of simulation. If simulator training applies to the event, then the applicable simulator(s) is/are listed in the "Simulation" section and the CRP for simulation training is given. This simulation training can either be used in place of live training, at the reduced CRP indicated; or can be used as a precursor training for the live event, i.e., weapons simulators, convoy trainers, observed fire trainers, etc. It is recommended that tasks be performed by simulation prior to being performed in a live-fire environment. However, in the case where simulation is used as a precursor for the live event, then the unit will receive credit for the live event CRP only. If a tactical situation develops that precludes performing the live event, the unit would then receive credit for the simulation CRP.

1014. MARINE CORPS GROUND T&R PROGRAM

1. The Marine Corps Ground T&R Program continues to evolve. The vision for Ground T&R Program is to publish a T&R Manual for every readiness-reporting unit so that core capability METs are clearly defined with supporting collective training standards, and to publish community-based T&R Manuals for all occupational fields whose personnel augment other units to increase their combat and/or logistic capabilities. The vision for this program includes plans to provide a Marine Corps training management information system that enables tracking of unit and individual training accomplishments by unit commanders and small unit leaders, automatically computing CRP for both units and individual Marines based upon MOS and rank (or billet). Linkage of T&R Events to the Marine Corps Task List (MCTL), through the core capability METs, has enabled objective assessment of training readiness in the DRRS.

2. DRRS measures and reports on the readiness of military forces and the supporting infrastructure to meet missions and goals assigned by the Secretary of Defense. With unit CRP based on the unit's training toward its METs, the CRP will provide a more accurate picture of a unit's readiness. This will give fidelity to future funding requests and factor into the allocation of resources. Additionally, the Ground T&R Program will help to ensure training remains focused on mission accomplishment and that training readiness reporting is tied to units' METLs.

GROUND SENSOR T&R MANUAL

CHAPTER 2

MISSION ESSENTIAL TASKS MATRIX

RESERVE FOR FUTURE USE.

GROUND SENSOR T&R MANUAL

CHAPTER 3

COLLECTIVE EVENTS

GROUND SENSOR T&R MANUAL

CHAPTER 3

COLLECTIVE EVENTS

3000. PURPOSE. This chapter includes all collective events. A collective event is an event that an established Ground Sensor element would perform. These events are linked to a Service-Level Mission Essential Task (MET). This linkage tailors collective and individual training for the selected MET. Each collective event is composed of component events that provide the major actions required. This may be likely actions, list of functions, or procedures. Accomplishment and proficiency level required of component events are determined by the event standard.

3001. ADMINISTRATIVE NOTES

1. T&R events are coded for ease of reference. Each event has a 4-4-4 character/digit identifier.

    a. The first four characters (or less) represent the community. This chapter contains the following community codes.

        GRSO - Ground Sensor Operator

    b. The second four characters represent the functional or duty area. This chapter contains the functional areas listed below.

        PLAN - Plan

    c. The last four digits represent the level (3000-9000) and sequence number (3001-9999) of the event. The GRSO collective events are separated into three levels (3000-5000).

        5000 - Platoon level events
        4000 - Section level events
        3000 - Team level events

3002. INDEX OF COLLECTIVE EVENTS BY FUNCTIONAL AREA

EVENT	DESCRIPTION	PAGE
	PLANNING	
GRSO-PLAN-3001	Conduct remote sensor operations	3-4
GRSO-PLAN-4001	Provide remote sensor support to MEB/Regimental operations	3-5
GRSO-PLAN-5001	Provide remote sensor support to MEF operations	3-6

3003. COLLECTIVE EVENTS

GRSO-PLAN-3001: Conduct remote sensor operations

SUPPORTED MET(S): 1

EVALUATION-CODED: YES   **SUSTAINMENT INTERVAL:** 6 months

DESCRIPTION: Ground sensor emplacement teams are to plan, coordinate, and execute remote sensor operations.

CONDITION: With the aid of references, given remote sensor equipment, and a requirement to employ remote sensors.

STANDARD: Ensuring the intelligence requirements are met, in a time limit established by the battle rhythm.

EVENT COMPONENTS:
1. Establish a monitoring site.
2. Make recommendations for the implantation of sensor operations to support the collection effort.
3. Prepare a sensor surveillance plan.
4. Conduct site reconnaissance.
5. Prepare sensor equipment
6. Establish communications link with the supported unit.
7. Execute sensor implant mission.
8. Monitor sensor activity.
9. Report sensor activity.
10. Execute sensor maintenance mission.
11. Execute sensor recovery mission.
12. Conduct preventative maintenance.

REFERENCES:
1. MCWP 3-40.3 Communications and Information Systems
2. MCRP 2-24B Remote Sensor Operations
3. TM 09856A-10/2C Sensor Mobile Monitor System AN/MSC-77
4. TM 10789A-14&P Ch 1 AN/GRQ-32 Radio Repeater Set
5. TM 11045A OI AN/PSQ-22 Hand Held Programmer Monitor
6. Command Standard Operating Procedures

GRSO-PLAN-4001: Provide remote sensor support to MEB/Regimental operations

SUPPORTED MET(S): 1

EVALUATION-CODED: YES   **SUSTAINMENT INTERVAL:** 12 months

DESCRIPTION: The section leader has to decide how best to employ Sensor Emplacement Teams in support of MEB/Regimental operations.

CONDITION: With the aid of references, given a mission, a sensor employment section, remote sensors with associated equipment, and a requirement to employ remote sensors.

STANDARD: For a duration established by the Commander, to satisfy the requirement for remote sensor support.

EVENT COMPONENTS:
1. Advise Commander on remote sensor capabilities and operations.
2. Determine support requirements.
3. Task organize sensor employment section.
4. Coordinate sensor frequency allocation with the communications officer.
5. Coordinate liaison with agencies/services/allies as required.
6. Provide reports as required.
7. Provide support to collections as required.

REFERENCES:
1. MCRP 2-24B Remote Sensor Operations
2. MCWP 2-2 MAGTF Intelligence Collections
3. TM 09632A-14&P/1 AN/GSQ-257 TRSS UGSS ENC-TRNS
4. TM 09855A-10/1B Tactical Remote Sensor Systems
5. TM 09856A-10/2C Sensor Mobile Monitor System AN/MSC-77
6. TM 10789A-14&P Ch 1 AN/GRQ-32 Radio Repeater Set
7. TM 11045A OI AN/PSQ-22 Hand Held Programmer Monitor
8. TM 11046A OI AN/PSQ-21 Imager
9. TM 8I759C OI Encoder Transmitter Unit, Version II
10. Command Embarkation Regulations
11. Command Standard Operating Procedures

GRSO-PLAN-5001: Provide remote sensor support to MEF operations

SUPPORTED MET(S): 1

EVALUATION-CODED: YES   **SUSTAINMENT INTERVAL:** 12 months

DESCRIPTION: This is a shared event between Ground Sensor Platoon Commanders and Platoon Sergeants to decide how best to employ Sensor Emplacement Teams in support of MEF operations.

CONDITION: With the aid of references, given a mission, a Ground Sensor Platoon element, remote sensors with associated equipment, and a requirement to employ remote sensors.

STANDARD: For a duration established by the Commander, to satisfy the requirement for remote sensor support.

EVENT COMPONENTS:
1. Advise Commander on remote sensor capabilities and operations.
2. Determine support requirements.
3. Task organize Ground Sensor Platoon (GSP) elements.
4. Coordinate sensor frequency allocation with the communications officer.

5. Coordinate liaison with agencies/services/allies as required.
6. Provide reports as required.
7. Provide support to collections as required.

REFERENCES:
1. MCRP 2-24B Remote Sensor Operations
2. MCWP 2-2 MAGTF Intelligence Collections
3. TM 09632A-14&P/1 AN/GSQ-257 TRSS UGSS ENC-TRNS
4. TM 09855A-10/1B Tactical Remote Sensor Systems
5. TM 09856A-10/2C Sensor Mobile Monitor System AN/MSC-77
6. TM 10789A-14&P Ch 1 AN/GRQ-32 Radio Repeater Set
7. TM 11045A OI AN/PSQ-22 Hand Held Programmer Monitor
8. TM 11046A OI AN/PSQ-21 Imager
9. TM 8I759C OI Encoder Transmitter Unit, Version II
10. Command Embarkation Regulations
11. Command Standard Operating Procedures

NAVMC 3500.17A
8 Sep 2010

GROUND SENSOR T&R MANUAL

CHAPTER 4

MOS 8621 INDIVIDUAL EVENTS

GROUND SENSOR T&R MANUAL

CHAPTER 4

MOS 8621 INDIVIDUAL EVENTS

4000. PURPOSE. This chapter details the individual events that pertain to MOS 8621, Sensor Surveillance Operator. These events are linked to a service-level Mission Essential Tasks (MET). This link tailors individual training for the selected MET. Each individual event provides an event title, along with the conditions events will be performed under, and the standard to which the event must be performed to be successful.

4001. ADMINISTRATIVE NOTES

1. T&R events are coded for ease of reference. Each event has a 4-4-4 character/digit identifier.

    a. The first four characters (or less) represent the community. This chapter contains the following community codes.

       8621 - Sensor Surveillance Operator

    b. The second four characters (or less) represent the functional or duty area. This chapter contains the functional areas listed below.

       DISS - Dissemination
       PLAN - Planning
       RESO - Remote Sensor Operations
       COMM - Communications
       SCTY - Security

    c. The last four digits represent (or less) the level (1000, 2000) and sequence number (1001-1999) of the event. The 8621 individual events are separated into two levels.

       1000 - Core
       2000 - Core Plus Skills

4002. INDEX OF INDIVIDUAL EVENTS BY LEVEL

EVENT	DESCRIPTION	PAGE
1000-LEVEL EVENTS		
	DISSEMINATION	
8621-DISS-1001	Write Joint Remote Sensor Reports (JRSR)	4-4
8621-DISS-1002	Conduct remote sensor(s) activity brief	4-4
	PLANNING	
8621-PLAN-1011	Prepare a sensor surveillance plan	4-5
8621-PLAN-1012	Utilize Sensor Surveillance planning cycle	4-6
	REMOTE SENSOR OPERATIONS	
8621-RESO-1016	Prepare remote sensor equipment for emplacement	4-7
8621-RESO-1017	Tactically Employ remote sensor equipment in daylight operations	4-8
8621-RESO-1018	Tactically Employ remote sensor equipment in night time operations	4-8
8621-RESO-1019	Tactically Conduct Maintenance on employed remote senor equipment in daylight operations	4-9
8621-RESO-1020	Tactically Conduct Maintenance on employed remote senor equipment in night time operations	4-10
8621-RESO-1024	Prepare remote sensor operator workstation(s)	4-11
8621-RESO-1025	Configure the mobile sensor monitoring system	4-11
8621-RESO-1026	Utilize the Hand Held program monitor (HHPM)	4-12
8621-RESO-1027	Analyze remote sensor data	4-13
8621-RESO-1028	Tactically Recover remote sensor equipment in daylight operations	4-14
8621-RESO-1029	Tactically Recover remote sensor equipment in night time operations	4-15
8621-RESO-1030	Conduct preventative maintenance	4-16
2000-LEVEL EVENTS		
	DISSEMINATION	
8621-DISS-2001	Conduct GSP capabilities brief	4-17
	COMMUNICATIONS	
8621-COMM-2011	Operate tactical communications equipment	4-18
	SECURITY	
8621-SCTY-2021	Handle classified material	4-18

4003. 1000-LEVEL EVENTS

8621-DISS-1001: Write Joint Remote Sensor Reports (JRSR)

EVALUATION-CODED: NO   **SUSTAINMENT INTERVAL:** 3 months

DESCRIPTION: Marine is required to provide Joint Remote Sensor Reports (JRSR) to supported unit(s) as required.

MOS PERFORMING: 8621

BILLETS: Surveillance Sensor Operator

GRADES: PVT, PFC, LCPL, CPL, SGT, SSGT, GYSGT, MSGT

INITIAL TRAINING SETTING: FORMAL

CONDITION: With the aid of references, given the requirement, a mission and sensor data.

STANDARD: Utilizing the correct format and sensor activation data in accordance with the supported units reporting requirements.

PERFORMANCE STEPS:
1. Determine which type of JRSR is to be used.
2. Assemble the data.
3. Insert data into prescribed format.
4. Submit the completed Reports.

REFERENCES:
1. MCRP 2-24B Remote Sensor Operations
2. MCWP 2-2 MAGTF Intelligence Collections
3. Command Standard Operating Procedures

8621-DISS-1002: Conduct remote sensor(s) activity brief

EVALUATION-CODED: NO   **SUSTAINMENT INTERVAL:** 6 months

DESCRIPTION: Marine requires a detailed understanding of the analysis behind determining valid sensor activity, and must be able to explain what the remote sensor activity means. Marine requires knowledge of proper briefing techniques as well as Microsoft Office suite.

MOS PERFORMING: 8621

BILLETS: GSP Team Leader, Section Leader, Platoon chief, Platoon Sgt, Platoon Commander

GRADES: PVT, PFC, LCPL, CPL, SGT, SSGT, GYSGT, MSGT

INITIAL TRAINING SETTING: FORMAL

CONDITION: With the aid of references, given a requirement, remote sensor reports, and presentation materials.

STANDARD: To provide intelligence information in support of the mission requirement in a time limit established by the Commanding Officer.

PERFORMANCE STEPS:
1. Research topic (utilize allsource information).
2. Develop an outline.
3. Identify specific mission requirements.
4. Develop media (w/speaker notes) adhering to classification guidance.
5. Maintain source data.
6. Conduct rehearsal.
7. Prepare briefing area.
8. Conduct brief.
9. Answer questions.

REFERENCES:
1. MCRP 2-24B Remote Sensor Operations
2. MCWP 2-2 MAGTF Intelligence Collections
3. MCRP 5-12C Operational Terms and Graphics
4. Command Standard Operating Procedures

8621-PLAN-1011: Prepare a sensor surveillance plan

EVALUATION-CODED: NO   **SUSTAINMENT INTERVAL:** 3 months

DESCRIPTION: The Sensor Surveillance Plan, when completed, will become Tab (b) to Appendix (11) (Surveillance and Reconnaissance) to Annex B (Intelligence) to the Operation Order.

MOS PERFORMING: 8621

BILLETS: GSP Team Leader, Section Leader, Platoon chief, Platoon Sgt, Platoon Commander

GRADES: PVT, PFC, LCPL, CPL, SGT, SSGT, GYSGT, MSGT

INITIAL TRAINING SETTING: FORMAL

CONDITION: With the aid of references, given the requirement, and the collections plan.

STANDARD: In a time limit established by the collections plan, ensuring the best possible sensor coverage of an area.

PERFORMANCE STEPS:
1. Review the Concept of Operations.
2. Review the Force List.
3. Review the Collection Plan.
4. Conduct a Terrain Study.
5. Conduct Feasibility Assessment.
6. Select remote sensor equipment as required.

7. Coordinate sensor frequency allocation with the communications officer.
8. Write the Sensor Surveillance Plan.
9. Brief Sensor Surveillance Plan.
10. Submit plan to the intelligence officer.

REFERENCES:
1. MCRP 2-24B Remote Sensor Operations
2. MCWP 2-2 MAGTF Intelligence Collections
3. MCRP 5-12C Operational Terms and Graphics
4. Command Standard Operating Procedures

8621-PLAN-1012: Utilize the sensor surveillance planning cycle

EVALUATION-CODED: NO   **SUSTAINMENT INTERVAL:** 3 months

DESCRIPTION: Marine must have a working knowledge of the sensor surveillance planning cycle and know how to incorporate into the intelligence cycle.

MOS PERFORMING: 8621

BILLETS: Sensor Surveillance operator

GRADES: PVT, PFC, LCPL, CPL, SGT, SSGT, GYSGT, MSGT

INITIAL TRAINING SETTING: FORMAL

CONDITION: With the aid of reference, given a mission.

STANDARD: Plan a sensor mission in accordance with MCRP 2-24B.

PERFORMANCE STEPS:
1. Conduct sensor employment IPB.
2. Determine asset availability.
3. Draft sensor surveillance plan.
4. Submit Draft sensor surveillance plan for approval.
5. Complete sensor surveillance plan.
6. Determine information collections requirements.

REFERENCES:
1. MCRP 2-24B Remote Sensor Operations
2. MCWP 2-2 MAGTF Intelligence Collections
3. MCRP 5-12C Operational Terms and Graphics
4. Command Standard Operating Procedures

8621-RESO-1021: Prepare remote sensor equipment for emplacement

EVALUATION-CODED: NO   **SUSTAINMENT INTERVAL:** 3 months

DESCRIPTION: Marine must prepare, program, and function check remote sensor equipment, to ensure operability prior to emplacing the remote sensor.

MOS PERFORMING: 8621

BILLETS: Surveillance Sensor Operator

GRADES: PVT, PFC, LCPL, CPL, SGT, SSGT, GYSGT, MSGT

INITIAL TRAINING SETTING: FORMAL

CONDITION: Without the aid of references, given remote sensor equipment, and a mission.

STANDARD: Ensuring remote sensor equipment is in operational condition, in order to support the assigned mission.

PERFORMANCE STEPS:
1. Visually/physically inspect remote sensor equipment for serviceability.
2. Program remote sensor equipment.
3. Assemble major components.
4. Perform a functions check on all remote sensor equipment.
5. Record program information.

REFERENCES:
1. TM 09632A-14P/1 Unattended Ground Sensor Set
2. TM 09855A-10/1B Tactical Remote Sensor Systems
3. TM 11045A OI AN/PSQ-22 Hand Held Programmer Monitor
4. TM 11046A OI AN/PSQ-21 Imager
5. TM 8I759C OI Encoder Transmitter Unit, Version II

8621-RESO-1017: Tactically employ remote sensor equipment during daylight operations

EVALUATION-CODED: NO   SUSTAINMENT INTERVAL: 3 months

DESCRIPTION: Marine must be able to locate the designated implant site and conceal the remote sensor to a degree that it is not easily discovered or located by the target to be collected on.

MOS PERFORMING: 8621

BILLETS: Surveillance Sensor Operator

GRADES: PVT, PFC, LCPL, CPL, SGT, SSGT, GYSGT, MSGT

INITIAL TRAINING SETTING: FORMAL

CONDITION: Without the aid of references, while wearing a combat load, given a mission, sensor surveillance plan, remote sensor equipment and associated mapping equipment.

STANDARD: Providing concealment of the sensor equipment and coverage of the overall objective.

PERFORMANCE STEPS:
1. Plot a geographic location.
2. Locate implant site(s).
3. Conduct Communications test
4. Emplace remote sensor(s).
5. Re-verify recorded program information.
6. Conceal the implant site.
7. Record remote sensor location.
8. Draw sketch map of senor location.
9. Draw sketch map of senor string location

REFERENCES:
1. FM 3-25.26 Map Reading and Land Navigation
2. MCRP 2-24B Remote Sensor Operations
3. TM 09632A-14&P/1 AN/GSQ-257 TRSS UGSS ENC-TRNS
4. TM 09855A-10/1B Tactical Remote Sensor Systems
5. TM 11045A OI AN/PSQ-22 Hand Held Programmer Monitor
6. TM 11046A OI AN/PSQ-21 Imager
7. TM 8I759C OI Encoder Transmitter Unit, Version II
8. Command Standard Operating Procedures
9. TM 10789A-14&P Ch 1 AN/GRQ-32 Radio Repeater Set

8621-RESO-1018: Tactically employ remote sensor equipment during Night time operations

EVALUATION-CODED: NO   **SUSTAINMENT INTERVAL:** 3 months

DESCRIPTION: Marine must be able to locate the designated implant site and conceal the remote sensor to a degree that it is not easily discovered or located by the target to be collected on during night time operations.

MOS PERFORMING: 8621

BILLETS: Surveillance Sensor Operator

GRADES: PVT, PFC, LCPL, CPL, SGT, SSGT, GYSGT, MSGT

INITIAL TRAINING SETTING: FORMAL

CONDITION: Without the aid of references, while wearing a combat load, during a low light/no light environment, given a mission, sensor surveillance plan, remote sensor equipment, Night optics and associated mapping equipment.

STANDARD: Providing concealment of the sensor equipment and coverage of the overall objective.

PERFORMANCE STEPS:
1. Plot a geographic location.
2. Prepare night optics.
3. Locate implant site(s) using night optics.
4. Conduct Communications test.
5. Emplace remote sensor(s).
6. Re-verify recorded program information.

7. Conceal the implant site.
8. Record remote sensor location.
9. Draw sketch map of senor location.
10. Draw sketch map of senor string location.

REFERENCES:
1. FM 3-25.26 Map Reading and Land Navigation
2. MCRP 2-24B Remote Sensor Operations
3. TM 09632A-14&P/1 AN/GSQ-257 TRSS UGSS ENC-TRNS
4. TM 09855A-10/1B Tactical Remote Sensor Systems
5. TM 11045A OI AN/PSQ-22 Hand Held Programmer Monitor
6. TM 11046A OI AN/PSQ-21 Imager
7. TM 8I759C OI Encoder Transmitter Unit, Version II
8. Command Standard Operating Procedures
9. TM 10789A-14&P Ch 1 AN/GRQ-32 Radio Repeater Set
10. TM 102 71A-23&P/2 AN/PUS-14's
11. TM 11-5855-262-10-02 AN/PUS-7B

8621-RESO-1019: Tactically Conduct Maintenance on employed remote senor equipment in daylight operations

EVALUATION-CODED: NO   **SUSTAINMENT INTERVAL:** 3 months

DESCRIPTION: Marine must be able to conduct a tactical battery change, re-conceal the implant site, trouble shoot programming, and adjust sensor coverage.

MOS PERFORMING: 8621

BILLETS: Surveillance Sensor Operator

GRADES: PVT, PFC, LCPL, CPL, SGT, SSGT, GYSGT, MSGT

INITIAL TRAINING SETTING: FORMAL

CONDITION: Without the aid of references, while wearing a combat load, given a sensor surveillance plan, sketch maps, remote sensor equipment and associated mapping equipment.

STANDARD: Ensuring all sensors are operational, concealed, and the coverage of the overall objective is obtained.

PERFORMANCE STEPS:
1. Locate the implant site.
2. Remove the remote sensor from the implant site.
3. Conduct appropriate maintenance.
4. Emplace remote sensor(s).
5. Re-verify recorded program information.
6. Conceal the implant site.

REFERENCES:
1. FM 3-25.26 Map Reading and Land Navigation
2. MCRP 2-24B Remote Sensor Operations

3. TM 09632A-14&P/1 AN/GSQ-257 TRSS UGSS ENC-TRNS
4. TM 09855A-10/1B Tactical Remote Sensor Systems
5. TM 11045A OI AN/PSQ-22 Hand Held Programmer Monitor
6. TM 11046A OI AN/PSQ-21 Imager
7. TM 8I759C OI Encoder Transmitter Unit, Version II
8. Command Standard Operating Procedures
9. TM 10789A-14&P Ch 1 AN/GRQ-32 Radio Repeater Set

8621-RESO-1020: Tactically Conduct Maintenance on employed remote senor equipment in nighttime operations

EVALUATION-CODED: NO   **SUSTAINMENT INTERVAL**: 3 months

DESCRIPTION: Marine must be able to conduct a tactical battery change, re-conceal the implant site, trouble shoot programming, and adjust sensor coverage.

MOS PERFORMING: 8621

BILLETS: Surveillance Sensor Operator

GRADES: PVT, PFC, LCPL, CPL, SGT, SSGT, GYSGT, MSGT

INITIAL TRAINING SETTING: FORMAL

CONDITION: Without the aid of references, while wearing a combat load, during a low light/no light environment, given a mission, sensor surveillance plan, remote sensor equipment, night optics, sketch maps, and associated mapping equipment.

STANDARD: Ensuring all sensors are operational concealed, and the coverage of the overall objective is obtained.

PERFORMANCE STEPS:
1. Prepare night optics.
2. Locate the implant site.
3. Remove the remote sensor from the implant site.
4. Conduct appropriate maintenance.
5. Emplace remote sensor(s).
6. Re-verify recorded program information.
7. Conceal the implant site.

REFERENCES:
1. FM 3-25.26 Map Reading and Land Navigation
2. MCRP 2-24B Remote Sensor Operations
3. TM 09632A-14&P/1 AN/GSQ-257 TRSS UGSS ENC-TRNS
4. TM 09855A-10/1B Tactical Remote Sensor Systems
5. TM 11045A OI AN/PSQ-22 Hand Held Programmer Monitor
6. TM 11046A OI AN/PSQ-21 Imager
7. TM 8I759C OI Encoder Transmitter Unit, Version II
8. Command Standard Operating Procedures

9. TM 10789A-14&P Ch 1 AN/GRQ-32 Radio Repeater Set
10. TM 102 71A-23&P/2 AN/PUS-14's
11. TM 11-5855-262-10-02 AN/PUS-7B

8621-RESO-1024: Prepare remote sensor operator workstation(s)

EVALUATION-CODED: NO   **SUSTAINMENT INTERVAL**: 3 months

DESCRIPTION: Marine will use a remote sensor operator workstation on a daily basis while conducting remote sensor operations. Marine is required to know how to install and operate the workstations software to perform their duties.

MOS PERFORMING: 8621

BILLETS: Surveillance Sensor Operator

GRADES: PVT, PFC, LCPL, CPL, SGT, SSGT, GYSGT, MSGT

INITIAL TRAINING SETTING: FORMAL

CONDITION: With the aid of references, given a remote sensor operator workstation, and application software.

STANDARD: Ensure application software is installed, map data is loaded, and the system is functioning as designed.

PERFORMANCE STEPS:
1. Review installation instructions.
2. Install Operating System (OS) software.
3. Verify operation of software components.
4. Load mapping data.
5. Utilize system.

REFERENCES:
1. FM 3-25.26 Map Reading and Land Navigation
2. MCRP 2-24B Remote Sensor Operations
3. TM 09856A-10/2C Sensor Mobile Monitor System AN/MSC-77
4. AIS Operating System Administrator Manual(s)
5. AIS System Manual
6. AIS System Operator's Manual

8621-RESO-1025: Configure the mobile sensor monitoring system

EVALUATION-CODED: NO   **SUSTAINMENT INTERVAL**: 3 months

DESCRIPTION: Marine must be able to configure a mobile sensor monitoring system to communicate with remote sensors and associated equipment.

MOS PERFORMING: 8621

BILLETS: Surveillance Sensor Operator

GRADES: PVT, PFC, LCPL, CPL, SGT, SSGT, GYSGT, MSGT

INITIAL TRAINING SETTING: FORMAL

CONDITION: With the aid of references, given a mobile sensor monitoring system and the requirement to conduct monitoring operations, and a sensor surveillance plan.

STANDARD: Ensuring communication with all equipment.

PERFORMANCE STEPS:
1. Ground system.
2. Visually/physically inspect mobile sensor monitoring system for serviceability.
3. Provide power to monitoring equipment.
4. Setup antennas.
5. Program sensor monitoring equipment.
6. Establish communications link with the supported unit.
7. Operate Environmental Control Unit (ECU).

REFERENCES:
1. MCWP 3-40.3 Communications and Information Systems
2. MCRP 2-24B Remote Sensor Operations
3. TM 09856A-10/2C Sensor Mobile Monitor System AN/MSC-77
4. AIS Operating System Administrator Manual(s)
5. AIS System Manual
6. AIS System Operator's Manual
7. Command Standard Operating Procedures

8621-RESO-1026: Utilize the Handheld program monitor

EVALUATION-CODED: NO   SUSTAINMENT INTERVAL: 3 months

DESCRIPTION: Marines will use the handheld program monitor to program sensor equipment, monitor sensor activations, record sensor locations, conduct communications test, and assist in the recovery of sensor equipment.

MOS PERFORMING: 8621

BILLETS: Surveillance Sensor Operator

GRADES: PVT, PFC, LCPL, CPL, SGT, SSGT, GYSGT, MSGT

INITIAL TRAINING SETTING: FORMAL

CONDITION: With the aid of references, given a Handheld program monitor, and a sensor plan.

STANDARD: Ensuring communication with all equipment and all sensor locations are recorded, in a time limit established by the mission Commander.

PERFORMANCE STEPS:
1. Ensure the handheld program monitor is programmed to the appropriate settings.
2. Utilize GPS function.
3. Analyze remote sensor data.
4. Report valid remote sensor data.

REFERENCES:
1. TM 09855A-10/1B Tactical Remote Sensor Systems
2. TM 11045A OI AN/PSQ-22 Hand Held Programmer Monitor

8621-RESO-1027: Analyze remote sensor data

EVALUATION-CODED: NO   **SUSTAINMENT INTERVAL:** 6 months

DESCRIPTION: Marine will analyze data received from remote sensors to evaluate valid activity near remote sensor(s).

MOS PERFORMING: 8621

BILLETS: Surveillance Sensor Operator

GRADES: PVT, PFC, LCPL, CPL, SGT, SSGT, GYSGT, MSGT

INITIAL TRAINING SETTING: FORMAL

CONDITION: Without the aid of references, given sensor monitoring equipment, and remote sensor data.

STANDARD: To report valid sensor activity, in a timeline established by the battle rhythm.

PERFORMANCE STEPS:
1. Identify remote sensor activation pattern(s).
2. Submit sensor report.
3. Maintain a journal.

REFERENCES:
1. FM 3-25.26 Map Reading and Land Navigation
2. MCRP 2-24B Remote Sensor Operations
3. TM 09632A-14&P/1 AN/GSQ-257 TRSS UGSS ENC-TRNS
4. TM 09856A-10/2C Sensor Mobile Monitor System AN/MSC-77
5. TM 11045A OI AN/PSQ-22 Hand Held Programmer Monitor

8621-RESO-1028: Recover remote sensor equipment in daylight operations

EVALUATION-CODED: NO   **SUSTAINMENT INTERVAL:** 3 months

DESCRIPTION: Marine will recover remote sensors once mission requirements have expired.

MOS PERFORMING: 8621

BILLETS: Surveillance Sensor Operator

GRADES: PVT, PFC, LCPL, CPL, SGT, SSGT, GYSGT, MSGT

INITIAL TRAINING SETTING: FORMAL

CONDITION: Without the aid of references, while wearing a combat load, given a mission, sensor surveillance plan, sketch maps, and associated mapping equipment.

STANDARD: Ensuring all equipment is recovered, in a time limit established by the mission Commander.

PERFORMANCE STEPS:
1. Locate the implant site.
2. Remove the remote sensor from the implant site.
3. Conceal implant site.
4. Disassemble the sensor for transport.

REFERENCES:
1. FM 3-25.26 Map Reading and Land Navigation
2. MCRP 2-24B Remote Sensor Operations
3. TM 09632A-14&P/1 AN/GSQ-257 TRSS UGSS ENC-TRNS
4. TM 09855A-10/1B Tactical Remote Sensor Systems
5. TM 11045A OI AN/PSQ-22 Hand Held Programmer Monitor
6. TM 11046A OI AN/PSQ-21 Imager
7. TM 8I759C OI Encoder Transmitter Unit, Version II
8. TM 10789A-14&P CH 1 AN/GRQ-32 Radio Repeater Set
9. Command Standard Operating Procedures

8621-RESO-1029: Recover remote sensor equipment in nighttime operations

EVALUATION-CODED: NO   SUSTAINMENT INTERVAL: 3 months

DESCRIPTION: Marine will recover remote sensors once mission requirements have expired.

MOS PERFORMING: 8621

BILLETS: Surveillance Sensor Operator

GRADES: PVT, PFC, LCPL, CPL, SGT, SSGT, GYSGT, MSGT

INITIAL TRAINING SETTING: FORMAL

CONDITION: Without the aid of references, while wearing a combat load, during a low light/ no light environment, given a mission, sensor surveillance plan, sketch maps, night optics, and associated mapping equipment.

STANDARD: Ensuring all equipment is recovered, in a time limit established by the mission Commander.

PERFORMANCE STEPS:
1. Prepare night optics.
2. Locate the implant site.
3. Remove the remote sensor from the implant site.
4. Conceal implant site.
5. Disassemble the sensor for transport.

REFERENCES:
1. FM 3-25.26 Map Reading and Land Navigation
2. MCRP 2-24B Remote Sensor Operations
3. TM 09632A-14&P/1 AN/GSQ-257 TRSS UGSS ENC-TRNS
4. TM 09855A-10/1B Tactical Remote Sensor Systems
5. TM 11045A OI AN/PSQ-22 Hand Held Programmer Monitor
6. TM 11046A OI AN/PSQ-21 Imager
7. TM 8I759C OI Encoder Transmitter Unit, Version II
8. TM 10789A-14&P CH 1 AN/GRQ-32 Radio Repeater Set
9. Command Standard Operating Procedures
10. TM 102 71A-23&P/2 AN/PUS-14's
11. TM 11-5855-262-10-02 AN/PUS-7B

8621-RESO-1030: Conduct preventative maintenance

EVALUATION-CODED: NO   SUSTAINMENT INTERVAL: 6 months

DESCRIPTION: Marine will perform operator maintenance on remote sensor equipment prior to and immediately after remote sensor equipment has been used to extend the service life of the remote sensor equipment.

MOS PERFORMING: 8621

BILLETS: Surveillance Sensor Operator

GRADES: PVT, PFC, LCPL, CPL, SGT, SSGT, GYSGT, MSGT

INITIAL TRAINING SETTING: FORMAL

CONDITION: With the aid of references, given remote sensor equipment requiring preventative maintenance, and preventative maintenance gear.

STANDARD: Ensure all items on the preventative maintenance check list are complete.

PERFORMANCE STEPS:
1. Adhere to all safety procedures.
2. Adhere to all hazardous material handling procedures.
3. Perform first echelon equipment maintenance.
4. Ensure SL 1-2-3 inventory is conducted.
5. Ensure operational checks are conducted.
6. Complete equipment records.
7. Report discrepancies.

REFERENCES:
1. TM 09632A-14&P/1 AN/GSQ-257 TRSS UGSS ENC-TRNS

2. TM 09856A-10/2C Sensor Mobile Monitor System AN/MSC-77
3. TM 10789A-14&P Ch 1 AN/GRQ-32 Radio Repeater Set
4. TM 11045A OI AN/PSQ-22 Hand Held Programmer Monitor
5. TM 11046A OI AN/PSQ-21 Imager
6. TM 11092A OI/A Maintenance Kit, Electronic Equipment for the Tactical Remote Sensor Systems, MK-3002/U
7. TM 4700-15/1 Marine Corps Ground Equipment Record Procedures
8. TM 8I759C OI Encoder Transmitter Unit, Version II
9. Command Standard Operating Procedures

4004. 2000-LEVEL EVENTS

8621-DISS-2001: Conduct GSP capabilities brief

EVALUATION-CODED: No   **SUSTAINMENT INTERVAL:** 6 months

DESCRIPTION: Marine requires knowledge of remote sensor operations, proper briefing techniques, and Microsoft Office suite.

MOS PERFORMING: 8621

BILLETS: Platoon Commander, Platoon Sergeant, Sensor Emplacement Team Leader

GRADES: CPL, SGT, SSGT, GYSGT, MSGT

INITIAL TRAINING SETTING: MOJT

CONDITION: With the aid of references, given sensor equipment, and presentation materials.

STANDARD: To inform requesting units of the key capabilities of a Sensor Emplacement Team, Section, Platoon, in a time limit established by the requesting unit.

PERFORMANCE STEPS:
1. State the mission of ground sensor emplacement teams.
2. State how a ground Sensor Emplacement Team can support the unit.
3. Identify each sensor capability.
4. State GSPs role in MASINT concepts.
5. Reference successful missions of GSP.
6. Answer questions.

REFERENCES:
1. MCRP 2-24B Remote Sensor Operations
2. MCWP 2-2 MAGTF Intelligence Collections
3. TM 09855A-10/1B Tactical Remote Sensor Systems
4. Command Standard Operating Procedures

8621-COMM-2011: Operate tactical communications equipment

EVALUATION-CODED: NO   **SUSTAINMENT INTERVAL:** 3 months

DESCRIPTION: Marine must be able to operate tactical communications equipment of multiple types.

MOS PERFORMING: 8621

BILLETS: Sensor Emplacement Team Leader, Surveillance Sensor Operator

GRADES: PVT, PFC, LCPL, CPL, SGT, SSGT, GYSGT, MSGT

INITIAL TRAINING SETTING: MOJT

CONDITION: With the aid of references, given tactical communication equipment, and the requirement to communicate.

STANDARD: to establish communications, in a time limit established by the battle rhythm.

PERFORMANCE STEPS:
1. Configure equipment for operation.
2. Conduct communications check.
3. Utilize proper communications procedures.

REFERENCES:
1. MCWP 3-40.3 Communications and Information Systems
2. TM 09856A-10/2C Sensor Mobile Monitor System AN/MSC-77
3. COMSEC Equipment Operator's Manual
4. Command Standard Operating Procedures

8621-SCTY-2021: Handle classified material

EVALUATION-CODED: NO   SUSTAINMENT INTERVAL: 6 months

DESCRIPTION: Marine must know how to handle classified material to prevent unauthorized disclosure since they are responsible for responsible for receiving, transferring, storing, and destroying their classified material.

MOS PERFORMING: 8621

BILLETS: Surveillance Sensor Operator

GRADES: PVT, PFC, LCPL, CPL, SGT, SSGT, GYSGT, MSGT

INITIAL TRAINING SETTING: MOJT

CONDITION: With the aid of references, given classified material(s), a government approved storage container, a method of destruction, and a logbook.

STANDARD: To ensure classified material is not compromised, and is 100% accounted for.

PERFORMANCE STEPS:
1. Secure item in a government approved safe.
2. Sign receipt card/book.
3. Mail card back to originator (applies only to cards).
4. Enter item into classified materials log book.
5. Notify CMCC to add material to CMCC inventory.

REFERENCES:
1. CSP 1 Cryptographic Security Policy and Procedures
2. DCID 1/14 Personnel Security Standards and Procedures Governing Eligibility for Access to Sensitive Compartmented Information
3. DCID 1/7 Security Controls on the Dissemination of Intelligence Information
4. DOD 5200.33R Defense Courier Service Regulations

5. OPNAVINST 5239.1 DON ADP Security Procedures
6. OPNAVINST 5510.1 Department of the Navy Information and Personnel Security Program Regulation
7. Command Procedures for Changing of Combinations
8. Command Standard Operating Procedures
9. Local Emergency Action Plan

APPENDIX A

ACRONYMS AND ABBREVIATIONS

AIS . . . . .Automated Intelligence Station
BMOS .Billet Military Occupational Specialty
CMS . . . . .COMSEC materials system
CMCC . . . . Classified Material Control Center
CO . . . . commanding officer
COMSEC . . . . .communications security
DoD . . . . .Department of Defense
DoDD . . . . .Department of Defense directive
DoDI . . . . .Department of Defense instruction
DON . . . . Department of the Navy
FMF . . . . Fleet Marine Force
FMFM . . . . .Fleet Marine Force manual
GPS . . . . .Global Positioning System
GSP . . . . .Ground Sensor Platoon
HQMC . . . . Headquarters, Marine Corps
JP . . . . .Joint publication
JRSR . . . . Joint Remote Sensor Report
MAGTF . . . . Marine air-ground task force
MARDIV . . . . .Marine Division
MARFOR . . . . .Marine Corps Forces
MCO . . . . Marine Corps Order
MCRP . . . . Marine Corps Readiness Publication
MCWP . . . . Marine Corps War fighting publication
MEF . . . . Marine Expeditionary Force
MEU . . . . .Marine Expeditionary Unit
MEU(SOC) . . . . Marine expeditionary unit (special operations capable)
MOJT . . . . Managed on the job training
MOS . . . . .military occupational specialty
NIPRNET . . . . .Non-secure internet protocol router network
OccFld . . . . .occupational field
OPLAN . . . . operation plan
OPORD . . . . operation order
OPSEC . . . . .operations security
S-2 . . . . intelligence staff officer
S-4 . . . . .logistics staff officer
S-6 . . . . communications and information systems staff officer
SES . . . . .Sensor Employment Squad
SET . . . . Sensor Employment Team
SIPRNET .secret internet protocol router network
SOP . . . . standing operating procedure
SPMAGTF . . . . special-purpose Marine air-ground task force
T/E . . . . table of equipment
T/O . . . . .table of organization
TRSS . . . . .Tactical Remote Sensor System
UGSS . . . . Unattended Ground Sensor Set

APPENDIX B

TERMS AND DEFINITIONS

Terms in this glossary are subject to change as applicable orders and directives are revised. Terms established by Marine Corps orders or directives take precedence after definitions found in Joint Pub 1-02, DOD Dictionary of Military and Associated Terms.

A

After Action Review. A professional discussion of training events conducted after all training to promote learning among training participants. The formality and scope increase with the command level and size of the training evolution. For longer exercises, they should be planned for at predetermined times during an exercise. The results of the AAR shall be recorded on an after action report and forwarded to higher headquarters. The commander and higher headquarters use the results of an AAR to reallocate resources, reprioritize their training plan, and plan for future training.

Assessment. An assessment is an informal judgment of the unit's proficiency and resources made by a commander or trainer to gain insight into the unit's overall condition. It serves as the basis for the midrange plan. Commanders make frequent use of these determinations during the course of the combat readiness cycle in order to adjust, prioritize or modify training events and plans.

C

Chaining. Chaining is a process that enables unit leaders to effectively identify subordinate collective events and individual events that support a specific collective event. For example, collective training events at the 4000-level are directly supported by collective events at the 3000-level. Utilizing the building block approach to progressive training, these collective events are further supported by individual training events at the 1000 and 2000-levels. When a higher-level event by its nature requires the completion of lower level events, they are "chained"; Sustainment credit is given for all lower level events chained to a higher event.

Collective Event. A collective event is a clearly defined, discrete, and measurable activity, action, or event (i.e., task) that requires organized team or unit performance and leads to accomplishment of a mission or function. A collective task is derived from unit missions or higher-level collective tasks. Task accomplishment requires performance of procedures composed of supporting collective or individual tasks. A collective task describes the exact performance a group must perform in the field under actual operational conditions. The term "collective" does not necessarily infer that a unit accomplishes the event. A unit, such as a squad or platoon conducting an attack; may accomplish a collective event or, it may be accomplished by an individual to accomplish a unit mission, such as a battalion supply officer completing a reconciliation of the battalion's CMR.

Thus, many collective events will have titles that are the same as individual events; however, the standard and condition will be different because the scope of the collective event is broader.

Collective Training Standards (CTS). Criteria that specify mission and functional area unit proficiency standards for combat, combat support, and combat service support units. They include tasks, conditions, standards, evaluator instruction, and key indicators. CTS are found within collective training events in T&R Manuals.

Combat Readiness Cycle. The combat readiness cycle depicts the relationships within the building block approach to training. The combat readiness cycle progresses from T&R Manual individual core skills training, to the accomplishment of collective training events, and finally, to a unit's participation in a contingency or actual combat. The combat readiness cycle demonstrates the relationship of core capabilities to unit combat readiness. Individual core skills training and the training of collective events lead to proficiency and the ability to accomplish the unit's stated mission.

Combat Readiness Percentage (CRP). The CRP is a quantitative numerical value used in calculating collective training readiness based on the E-Coded events that support the unit METL. CRP is a concise measure of unit training accomplishments. This numerical value is only a snapshot of training readiness at a specific time. As training is conducted, unit CRP will continuously change.

Component Events. Component events are the major tasks involved in accomplishing a collective event. Listing these tasks guide Marines toward the accomplishment of the event and help evaluators determine if the task has been done to standard. These events may be lower-level collective or individual events that must be accomplished.

Condition. The condition describes the training situation or environment under which the training event or task will take place. Expands on the information in the title by identifying when, where, and why the event or task will occur and what materials, personnel, equipment, environmental provisions, and safety constraints must be present to perform the event or task in a real-world environment. Commanders can modify the conditions of the event to best prepare their Marines to accomplish the assigned mission (e.g. in a desert environment; in a mountain environment; etc.).

Core Competency. Core competency is the comprehensive measure of a unit's ability to accomplish its assigned MET. It serves as the foundation of the T&R Program. Core competencies are those unit core capabilities and individual core skills that support the commander's METL and T/O mission statement. Individual competency is exhibited through demonstration of proficiency in specified core tasks and core plus tasks. Unit proficiency is measured through collective tasks.

Core Capabilities. Core capabilities are the essential functions a unit must be capable of performing during extended contingency/combat operations. Core unit capabilities are based upon mission essential tasks derived from operational plans; doctrine and established tactics; techniques and procedures.

Core Plus Capabilities. Core plus capabilities are advanced capabilities that are environment, mission, or theater specific. Core plus capabilities may entail high-risk, high-cost training for missions that are less likely to be assigned in combat.

Core Plus Skills. Core plus skills are those advanced skills that are environment, mission, rank, or billet specific. 2000-level training is designed to make Marines proficient in core skills in a specific billet or at a specified rank at the Combat Ready level. 3000-8000-level training produces combat leaders and fully qualified section members at the Combat Qualified level. Marines trained at the Combat Qualified level are those the commanding officer feels are capable of accomplishing unit-level missions and of directing the actions of subordinates. Many core plus tasks are learned via MOJT, while others form the base for curriculum in career level MOS courses taught by the formal school.

Core Skills. Core skills are those essential basic skills that "make" a Marine and qualify that Marine for an MOS. They are the 1000-level skills introduced in entry-level training at formal schools.

D

Defense Readiness Reporting System (DRRS). A comprehensive readiness reporting system that evaluates readiness on the basis of the actual missions and capabilities assigned to the forces. It is a capabilities-based, adaptive, near real-time reporting system for the entire Department of Defense.

Deferred Event. A T&R event that a commanding officer may postpone when in his or her judgment, a lack of logistic support, ammo, ranges, or other training assets requires a temporary exemption. CRP cannot be accrued for deferred "E-Coded" events.

Delinquent Event. An event becomes delinquent when a Marine or unit exceeds the sustainment interval for that particular event. The individual or unit must update the delinquent event by first performing all prerequisite events. When the unit commander deems that performing all prerequisite is unattainable, then the delinquent event will be re-demonstrated under the supervision of the appropriate evaluation authority.

E

E-Coded Event. An "E-Coded" event is a collective T&R event that is a noted indicator of capability or, a noted Collective skill that contributes to the unit's ability to perform the supported MET. As such, only "E-Coded" events are assigned a CRP value and used to calculate a unit's CRP.

Entry-level training. Pipeline training that equips students for service with the Marine Operating Forces.

Evaluation. Evaluation is a continuous process that occurs at all echelons, during every phase of training and can be both formal and informal. Evaluations ensure that Marines and units are capable of conducting their combat mission. Evaluation results are used to reallocate resources, reprioritize the training plan, and plan for future training.

Event (Training). (1) An event is a significant training occurrence that is identified, expanded and used as a building block and potential milestone for a unit's training. An event may include formal evaluations. (2) An event within the T&R Program can be an individual training evolution, a collective training evolution or both. Through T&R events, the unit commander ensures that individual Marines and the unit progress from a combat capable status to a Fully Combat Qualified (FCQ) status.

Event Component. Event components are the major procedures (i.e., actions) that must occur to perform a Collective Event to standard.

Exercise Commander (EC). The Commanding General, Marine Expeditionary Force or his appointee will fill this role, unless authority is delegated to the respective commander of the Division, Wing, or FSSG. Responsibilities and functions of the EC include: (1) designate unit(s) to be evaluated, (2) may designate an exercise director, (3) prescribe exercise objectives and T&R events to be evaluated, (4) coordinate with commands or agencies external to the Marine Corps and adjacent Marine Corps commands, when required.

Exercise Director (ED). Designated by the EC to prepare, conduct, and report all evaluation results. Responsibilities and functions of the ED include: (1) Publish a letter of instruction (LOI) that: delineates the T&R events to be evaluated, establishes timeframe of the exercise, lists responsibilities of various elements participating in the exercise, establishes safety requirements/guidelines, and lists coordinating instructions. (2) Designate the TEC and TECG to operate as the central control agency for the exercise. (3) Assign evaluators, to include the senior evaluator, and ensure that those evaluators are properly trained. (4) Develop the general exercise scenario taking into account any objectives/ events prescribed by the EC. (5) Arrange for all resources to include: training areas, airspace, aggressor forces, and other required support.

I

Individual Readiness. The individual training readiness of each Marine is measured by the number of individual events required and completed for the rank or billet currently held.

Individual Training. Training that applies to individual Marines. Examples include rifle qualifications and HMMWV driver licensing.

Individual Training Standards (ITS). Individual Training Standards specify training tasks and standards for each MOS or specialty within the Marine Corps. In most cases, once an MOS or community develops a T&R, the ITS order will be cancelled. However, most communities will probably fold a large portion of their ITS into their new T&R manual.

M

Marine Corps Ground Training and Readiness (T&R) Program. The T&R Program is the Marine Corps' primary tool for planning and conducting training, for planning and conducting training evaluation, and for assessing training readiness. The program will provide the commander with standardized programs of instruction for units within the ground combat, combat support, and combat service support communities. It consolidates the ITS, CTS, METL and other individual and unit training management tools. T&R is a program of standards that systematizes commonly accepted skills, is open to innovative change, and above all, tailors the training effort to the unit's mission. Further, T&R serves as a training guide and provides commanders an immediate assessment of unit combat readiness by assigning a CRP to key training events. In short, the T&R Program is a building block approach to training that maximizes flexibility and produces the best-trained Marines possible.

Mission Essential Task(s) MET(s). A MET is a collective task in which an organization must be proficient in order to accomplish an appropriate portion of its wartime mission(s). MET listings are the foundation for the T&R manual; all events in the T&R manual support a MET.

Mission Essential Task List (METL). Descriptive training document that provides units a clear, war fighting focused description of collective actions necessary to achieve wartime mission proficiency. The service-level METL, that which is used as the foundation of the T&R Manual, is developed using Marine Corps doctrine, Operational Plans, T/Os, UJTL, UNTL, and MCTL. For community based T&R Manuals, an occupational field METL is developed to focus the community's collective training standards. Commanders develop their unit METL from the service-level METL, operational plans, contingency plans, and SOPs.

O

Operational Readiness (DOD, NATO). OR is the capability of a unit/formation, ship, weapon system, or equipment to perform the missions or functions for which it is organized or designed. May be used in a general sense or to express a level or degree of readiness.

P

Performance step. Performance steps are included in the components of an Individual T&R Event. They are the major procedures (i.e., actions) a unit Marine must accomplish to perform an individual event to standard. They describe the procedure the task performer must take to perform the task under operational conditions and provide sufficient information for a task performer to perform the procedure (May necessitate identification of supporting steps, procedures, or actions in outline form.). Performance steps follow a logical progression and should be followed sequentially, unless otherwise stated. Normally, performance steps are listed only for 1000-level individual events (those that are taught in the entry-level MOS school).

Prerequisite Event. Prerequisites are the academic training and/or T&R events that must be completed prior to attempting the event.

R

Readiness (DOD). Readiness is the ability of US military forces to fight and meet the demands of the national military strategy. Readiness is the synthesis of two distinct but interrelated levels: (a) Unit readiness--The ability to provide capabilities required by combatant commanders to execute assigned missions. This is derived from the ability of each unit to deliver the outputs for which it was designed. (b) Joint readiness--The combatant commander's ability to integrate and synchronize ready combat and support forces to execute assigned missions.

S

Section Skill Tasks. Section Skills are those competencies directly related to unit functioning. They are group rather than individual in nature, and require participation by a section (S-1, S-2, S-3, etc).

Simulation Training. Simulators provide the additional capability to develop and hone core and core plus skills. Accordingly, the development of simulator training events for appropriate T&R syllabi can help maintain valuable combat resources while reducing training time and cost. Therefore, in cases where simulator fidelity and capabilities are such that simulator training closely matches that of actual training events, T&R Manual developers may include the option of using simulators to accomplish the training. CRP credit will be earned for E-Coded simulator events based on assessment of relative training event performance.

Standard. A standard is a statement that establishes criteria for how well a task or learning objective must be performed. The standard specifies how well, completely, or accurately a process must be performed or product produced. For higher-level collective events, it describes why the event is being done and the desired end-state of the event. Standards become more specific for lower-level events and outline the accuracy, time limits, sequencing, quality, product, process, restrictions, etc., that indicate the minimum acceptable level of performance required of the event. At a minimum, both collective and individual training standards consist of a task, the condition under which the task is to be performed, and the evaluation criteria that will be used to verify that the task has been performed to a satisfactory level.

Sustainment Training. Periodic retraining or demonstration of an event required maintaining the minimum acceptable level of proficiency or capability required to accomplish a training objective. Sustainment training goes beyond the entry-level and is designed to maintain or further develop proficiency in a given set of skills.

Systems Approach to Training (SAT). An orderly process for analyzing, designing, developing, implementing, and evaluating a unit's training program to ensure the unit, and the Marines of that unit acquire the knowledge and skills essential for the successful conduct of the unit's wartime missions.

T

Training Task. This describes a direct training activity that pertains to an individual Marine. A task is composed of 3 major components: a description of what is to be done, a condition, and a standard.

Technical Exercise Controller (TEC). The TEC is appointed by the ED, and usually comes from his staff or a subordinate command. The TEC is the senior evaluator within the TECG and should be of equal or higher grade than the commander(s) of the unit(s) being evaluated. The TEC is responsible for ensuring that the evaluation is conducted following the instructions contained in this order and MCO 1553.3B. Specific T&R Manuals are used as the source for evaluation criteria.

Tactical Exercise Control Group (TECG). A TECG is formed to provide subject matter experts in the functional areas being evaluated. The benefit of establishing a permanent TECG is to have resident, dedicated evaluation authority experience, and knowledgeable in evaluation technique. The responsibilities and functions of the TECG include: (1) developing a detailed exercise scenario to include the objectives and events prescribed by the EC/ED in the exercise LOI; (2) conducting detailed evaluator training prior to the exercise; (3) coordinating and controlling role players and aggressors; (4) compiling the evaluation data submitted by the evaluators and submitting required results to the ED; (5) preparing and conducting a detailed exercise debrief for the evaluated unit(s).

Training Plan. The training plan is a training document that outlines the general plan for the conduct of individual and collective training in an organization for specified periods of time.

U

Unit CRP. Unit CRP is a percentage of the E-coded collective events that support the unit METL accomplished by the unit. Unit CRP is the average of all MET CRP.

Unit Evaluation. All units in the Marine Corps must be evaluated, either formally or informally, to ensure they are capable of conducting their combat mission. Informal evaluations should take place during all training events. The timing of formal evaluations is critical and should, when appropriate, be directly related to the units' operational deployment cycle. Formal evaluations should take place after the unit has been staffed with the majority of its personnel, has had sufficient time to train to individual and collective standards, and early enough in the training cycle so there is sufficient time to correctly identified weaknesses prior to deployment. All combat units, and units task organized for combat require formal evaluations prior to operational deployments.

Unit Training Management (UTM). Unit training management is the use of the SAT and Marine Corps training principles in a manner that maximizes training results and focuses the training priorities of the unit on its wartime mission. UTM governs the major peacetime training activity of the Marine Corps and applies to all echelons of the Total Force.

W

Waived Event. An event that is waived by a commanding officer when in his or her judgment, previous experience or related performance satisfies the requirement of a particular event.

APPENDIX C

REFERENCES

Department of Defense (DOD)
5200.33R Defense Courier Service Regulations

Office of the Chief of Naval Operations Instruction (OPNAVINST)
5239.1 DON ADP Security Procedures
5510.1 Department of the Navy Information and Personnel Security Program Regulation

Marine Corps Requirement Publications (MCRP)
2-24B Remote Sensor Operations
5-12C Operational Terms and Graphics

Marine Corps Warfighting Publications (MCWPs)
2-2 MAGTF Intelligence Collections
3-40.3 Communications and Information Systems

Army Field Manual (FM)
3-25.26 Map Reading and Land Navigation

Director of Central Intelligence Directive (DCID)
1/14 Personnel Security Standards and Procedures Governing Eligibility for Access to Sensitive Compartmented Information
1/7 Security Controls on the Dissemination of Intelligence Information

Technical Manuals (TM)
102 71A-23&P/2 AN/PUS-14's
11-5855-262-10-02 AN/PUS-7B
09632A-14&P/1 AN/GSQ-257 TRSS UGSS ENC-TRNS
09855A-10/1B Tactical Remote Sensor Systems
11045A OI AN/PSQ-22 Hand Held Programmer Monitor
11046A OI AN/PSQ-21 Imager
8I759C OI Encoder Transmitter Unit, Version II
10789A-14&P Ch 1 AN/GRQ-32 Radio Repeater Set
09856A-10/2C Sensor Mobile Monitor System AN/MSC-77
11092A OI/A Maintenance Kit, Electronic Equipment for the Tactical Remote Sensor Systems, MK-3002/U
4700-15/1 Marine Corps Ground Equipment Record Procedures

Miscellaneous
Command Standard Operating Procedures
AIS Operating System Administrator Manual(s)
AIS System Manual
AIS System Operator's Manual
COMSEC Equipment Operator's Manual
Command Procedures for Changing of Combinations
Local Emergency Action Plan
CSP 1 Cryptographic Security Policy and Procedures